Devotions From a Woman's Heart

Deborah Andre

DEDICATION

This book is dedicated to my wonderful husband, Shelby,
who has provided me with the free time to complete this project.

I also dedicate it to my children and step-children,
Jamie, Patrick, Jason, Nicole and Joshua,
who have encouraged me to do this project.

I also want to dedicate it to my Heavenly Father
who has taught me so much as I have walked with Him
and learned from Him the many lessons described in this book.

Deborah Andre

ACKNOWLEDGEMENTS

I want to thank my husband, my sister-in-law, Carolyn Andre, my friend Carolyn Wells and my co-workers, Martha and Priscilla and for reading and helping me edit my book .

I am so thankful to have people in my life who love and support me as I publish my first book. May God Bless them and continue to use us all in our walk with Him.

Deborah Andre

CONTENTS

Devotions From a Woman's Heart

No Peace - Know Peace

This morning, as I woke up and made my coffee, I looked out the window and discovered it had snowed last night. We are in the dead of winter, and yet, today everything is covered with a beautiful layer of clean white snow. I pray, "Oh Lord, how beautiful, still, and quiet everything is this morning. How totally peaceful! How alive the dead of winter looks now. Why are our lives not filled with this perfect peace? Why are the winter of our minds not covered and washed as white as the snow?"

He replies to me, in His still quiet voice, in my mind, "It can my child! It can be this peaceful inside your deepest being."

A scripture, I read several years ago, rings so loudly in my mind. Deuteronomy 30:1-20. This book of the Bible was written by Moses to tell the children of Israel how they are to live once they enter the promise land. It is filled with many instructions and guidelines they are to follow. In verse 6 of chapter 30, Moses tells them:

"...*The Lord your God will circumcise your heart and the heart of your descendants, to love the Lord your God with all your heart and with all your soul, so that you may live.*"(NASB)

In Verses 19-20 it says:

"I call heaven and earth to witness against you today, that I have set before you life and death, the blessing and the curse. So choose life in order that you may live, you and your descendants, by loving the Lord your God, by obeying His voice, and by holding fast to Him; for this is your life and the length of your days, that you may live in the land which the Lord swore to your fathers, to Abraham, Isaac, and Jacob, to give them." (NASB)

You may be saying, "Well, that is all fine and good, but that was many, many years ago, and was spoken to the Jews who were God's chosen people. You are right in a way, but it still applies today to you and me.

In Matthew 11:28-30, Jesus has been trying to teach the religious leaders in Galilee and they are refusing to listen to Him. In verse 20, Jesus begins to denounce the cities where He has been performing miracles because they continue to deny who He is. He warns them of the coming judgement they will experience. The amazing part is His prayer to the Father in vs. 25.

"I praise You Father, Lord of heaven and earth, that You have hidden these things from the wise and intelligent and have revealed them to infants. Yes Father, for this way was well-pleasing in Your sight. All things have been handed over to Me by my Father and no one knows the Son except the Father; nor does anyone know the Father, except the Son, and anyone to whom the Son wills to reveal Him." (NASB)

Now here is our invitation to know the Father revealed to us through the Son (Jesus). *"Come to Me, all you who are weary and heavy-laden, and I will give you rest. Take my yoke upon you*

*and learn from Me, for I am gentle and humble in heart and you
will find rest for your souls. For My yoke is easy and My burden is
light."* (NASB)

Our invitation is to come to Jesus. He understands us. He
knows where we have been and where we are going. For you see,
Jesus is God, came in the flesh, in order to better understand
what you and I are going through. He never did anything wrong
(sin), yet He was stoned, thrown out of cities, ridiculed,
misunderstood, rejected by His own family and eventually
crucified for sins He never committed. He sees and knows
everything. He even knows the number of hairs on your head.
That is how much He knows and cares about you and me.

Hebrews 2:14-18 tell us,

*"Therefore, since the children share in flesh and blood, He Himself
likewise also partook of the same, that through death He might
render powerless him who had the power of death, that is, the
devil, and might free those who through fear of death were
subject to slavery all their lives. For assuredly He does not give
help to angels, but He gives help to the descendant of Abraham.
Therefore, He had to be made like His brethren in all things, so
that He might become a merciful and faithful high priest in things
pertaining to God, to make propitiation for the sins of the people.
For since He Himself was tempted in that which He has suffered,
He is able to come to the aid of those who are tempted."* (NASB)

You see, Jesus came to destroy the power of death that
burns in our hearts such as bitterness, anger, hurt, self-pity,
abuse, and anything else we hold on to. Satan wants us to believe

his lies about these things. He wants us to be miserable, and think we deserve to be miserable. But do we have to continue to believe these lies? NO! We just read that this is the very reason Jesus came, to destroy the power of death!

A few years ago I was teaching through the book of John, and that Jesus continually referred to us sheep. He said, *"My sheep hear My voice, they know Me and I know them and they follow me; I am the good Shepherd; the good Shepherd lays down His life for the sheep."* (John 10:27, 11 NASB)

One thing I have learned about studying God's word is that whenever a word or phrase is repeated, He is trying to make a point. So I decided that if I was a sheep, I needed to know something about them. So I went to the library and had them pull everything they could find about sheep. Guess what? Interestingly enough, they had a lot more information about goats than sheep. I told them I was not a goat but a sheep, so I took the information and found some very interesting things about sheep. Let's look at what I discovered and compare it to Psalms 23 (NASB).

Sheep are the dumbest animal God ever created. They have to have a shepherd to lead and protect them. They are unable to find green pastures on their own.
"The Lord is my shepherd, I shall not want.
He makes me lie down in green pastures."

Sheep are unable to drink from running water, even if they are dying of thirst.

"He leads me beside quiet waters."

Sheep must be protected from their enemies. They are incapable of defending themselves so they need a shepherd to protect them.

"He restores my soul;
He leads me in paths of righteousness for His name's sake.
Even though I walk through the valley of the shadow of
death I will fear no evil, for You are with me."

Sheep cannot be driven, they must be lead.
"Your rod and staff, they comfort me."

At night the shepherd gathers the sheep in an area made of thick briers and the shepherd will lay across the only way into the fold so that if an enemy comes it has to cross over the shepherd in order to get to the sheep
"You prepare a table before me in the presence of my enemies."

It is not uncommon for sheep to get a worm inside their head which drives them so crazy they will literally beat their head against a rock or a tree until they die.
"You anoint my head with oil;
My cup runneth over."

When a lamb continues to wander from the fold, the shepherd will literally break the lamb's leg, splint it, and place the lamb on his neck and carry it until the leg is healed. The lamb learns the shepherd so well that it never wanders away from the fold again.

"Surely, goodness and mercy will follow me
all the days of my life.
And I will dwell in the house of the Lord forever.

Oh how true and alive Psalms 23 becomes when we look at ourselves as sheep. I wonder how many times the Lord has had to break our legs in order to bring us to the point that we do not wander from the fold. You see, a root of bitterness will cause us to beat our heads against a wall too. Looking for peace against the running streams of anger, self-pity, and hurt feelings will cause us to die because of starvation spiritually and physically. But it does not have to be this way!

There is only one way to overcome this. I can not do it for you, and neither can anyone else. You alone can do exactly what we saw at the beginning to this devotion. Choose life that you may live. Love the Lord your God, listen to His voice, and hold fast to Him.

You see, you are only hurting yourself. You are right, no one feels your pain; no one knows or understands you, only God can do that. He sees and knows everything. Nothing is hidden from His face.

Jesus cries out to you, *"Come unto Me, all who are weary and heavy burdened..."* (NASB)
Is it really worth all the pain and misery you are going through?

Jesus says, *"The thief comes only to steal and kill and destroy; I came that they may have life, and have it abundantly."* (John 10:10 NASB) *"Peace I leave with you; My peace I give to you; Do not let your heart be troubled nor let it be fearful"* (John 14:27 NASB)

You may be saying, "That is all good and nice but I have tried it. It does not work."

Well, my friend, all I can do is say that it does work. You see, you must be willing to totally and completely with your whole heart, fall on your face and cry out to God in prayer, something like this.

"Oh Lord, I am tired of living this way. I am so tired of being tortured with my life, I am so tired of holding on to past hurts and bitterness, and I am so tired of trying to do it my way. I come to You now, I lay it all at the foot of the cross and I give it to You. Oh Lord, come into my life and give me the peace You talked about. Today, Oh Lord, I choose life. For the first time in my life, I choose to lay it all down and ask You to come in and take total control of me. Here I am Lord, if You are real, make Yourself real to me. I hold nothing back. I give it all to You."

If you choose to do this, I promise, oh the joy that will flood your soul. Oh the peace that passes all understanding. Oh the change that takes place deep inside you.

If you make this decision, what is the next step you need to take? Begin to study God's word, find a Bible believing church and share your decision with others. Follow in believer's baptism, which is the first step of obedience to Christ.

Now study and pray every day. Make it a priority in your life to know God and allow the Holy Spirit to reveal Himself to you. He will!

In John 14:15-27, Jesus telling His disciples that He will not leave them as orphans. Then He says , *"If you love Me, you will keep My commandments. I will ask the Father, and He will give you another Helper that He may be with you forever;..."* Then in verse 26 He said, *"But the Helper, the Holy Spirit, whom the Father will send in My name, He will teach you all things, and bring to your remembrance all that I said to you."* (NASB)

When our lives are changed, the Holy Spirit will lead us into all truth. It is His responsibility to teach us. All we have to do is ask Him; He will help us understand what the Word is saying and He will reveal it to us if we just listen. I challenge you today to try it.

"Oh Lord, may whoever reads this take it to heart. May You speak to their deep inner being and give them the desire to let go and let You have Your way in their life. Lord, I love you and Praise You for what you are going to do with this. May the peace and joy you have given me be passed to those who are willing to choose life, serve and follow You. Break off the pieces of bitterness and anger that has kept them in bondage for so many years, and release them Father to experience the Abundant Life only You give. Thank you Father for your faithfulness and mercy You will

disclose to them. In Jesus name I pray. A-Men"

May you Know Real Peace in your life!

Shifting Sand

Today, while lying on the beach writing in my journal, I cry out to the Lord for direction in my life. Fourteen months ago, my husband made his final journey to heaven, and my life is changed forever. I feel confused, lost, unable to decide what I am to do and where I am to go and just how I am to spend the rest of my life. I feel like a child, 14 years of age who, being pushed by the school system, tries to decide what career they want to have when they graduate. The only difference is that I am 51 years old and I thought my plot in life had been established. I was to grow old with my husband, enjoy our grandchild and live together until we are in our 80's serving the Lord in our local church. But now this dream will never happen. Now I just want to know what God has planned for me.

As I write in my journal, laying out all the options I have to the Lord, He begins to instruct me to play in the sand. That sounded like a strange request to me but I decided to just do it anyway. I began by digging a trench, just wondering what I was supposed to play. I remember as a child digging a hole for the frogs to hide in or so we thought we were doing that, so I began to dig. As I dug the sand was not cooperating; it just kept falling into my hole and would not stay back. As I continued to dig deeper and deeper I ran into some moist sand and that sand was a little easier to work with so I decided that God was showing me that the sand was my life and as I allowed the Holy Spirit to add moisture into my life, it would begin to take form and be more useful.

As I continued to dig and went up under the part that seemed to be holding up, eventually I hit a spot that contained dry sand and the whole thing would gradually begin to fall and eventually crash down upon my hand once again.

As I began to ask God what was going on He reminded me of a familiar scripture found in Matthew 7:24-27. Jesus had been teaching what is commonly referred to as "the Sermon on the Mount". He finished this teaching with these words:

"Therefore everyone who hears these words of Mine and acts on them, may be compared to a wise man who builds his house on the rock. And the rain fell, and the floods came, and the winds blew and slammed against that house; and yet it did not fall, for it had been founded on the rock. Everyone who hears these words of Mine and does not act on them, will be like a foolish man who built his house on the sand. The rain fell and the floods came and the winds blew and slammed against the house; and it fell—and great was its fall." (NASB)

Then it hit me, the moisture of the sand was not the Holy Spirit helping me but was my own effort trying to fix the problem.

As I added water to the dry sand, it appears to be holding up the walls of my life. As I continue to try and fix my problems and decide the direction for my life things will begin to take shape but will not last. Eventually rain will fall, winds will blow and my house will once again cave in.

I remember watching the waves yesterday as they came into the shore the sand was easily shifted and was caught up into the wave. Even as I stood on the sand that felt secure, whenever a wave would crash against the shore, the sand under my feet would slowly wash away and shift and eventually it buried my feet.

So it is with our life. If we try to fix our problems ourselves or try and figure out what we are to do or where we are to go, it may appear we have it all together for a short period of time but then it happens; wind, rain, problems and everything comes crashing down around us.

Another image came to my mind about that time. A couple days before I had been walking along the beach, enjoying the day and I came upon an area of beach that was made out of a rock ledge. As I stood and watched the wave's crash against it, the rock ledge did not move, unlike the sand on the beach that easily conformed to the waves.

As I sat there and pondered this revelation, I realized that God was telling me, unless I establish my life on Him, my Rock, my life will continue to shift, turn, and be confused and unsure. But if I will allow my life to be built upon Him, then it will not be moved. Just as scripture says, as I allow God's word to shape my life, it will not be moved.

Psalms 40:1-2 says, *"I waited patiently for the Lord; He turned to me and heard my cry. He lifted me out of the slimy pit, out of the mud and mire; He set my feet on a rock and gave me a firm place to stand."* (NIV)

So what do I need to do? I need to wait upon the Lord. Continue doing what I am doing right now until the Lord gives me clear direction about His plan for my life. I do not need to continue to ponder, worry or wonder. I need to just continue to study His word, write devotions like He has already shown me to do and continue to be content waiting patiently on Him.

I am reminded of an old hymn that goes like this:

"My hope is built on nothing less, than Jesus blood and righteousness; I dare not trust the sweetest frame, But wholly lean on Jesus name. When darkness seems to hide His face, I rest on His unchanging grace; in every high and stormy gale, my anchor holds within the veil. His oath, His covenant His blood supports me in the whelming flood; when all around my soul gives way, He then is all my hope and stay. When He shall come with trumpet sound, Oh, may I then in Him be found; Dressed in His righteousness alone, faultless to stand before the throne. On

Christ, the solid Rock, I stand; All other ground is sinking sand, All other ground is sinking sand." (Baptist Hymnal, "The Solid Rock")

Oh if we could only believe and totally trust these words. If we could ever get a hold of the fact that as long as we are trying to fix our life, adding our input and thinking we are OK until the storm comes. If we could just wait upon the Lord as David told us in Psalms and allow God's word to become real to us how much better off we would be.

Oh Lord, Help us today to wait upon You. Help us to remember to allow your word to penetrate our hearts and change us and make us useful in Your hands. Help us to remember that as long as we try to fix things our foundation is never secure. Help us to allow you to build our life on the Rock of Jesus that never changes. In Jesus Name!

A Lesson from the Waves

Today I sit on the beach listening to the waves as they crash against the shore. The wind is blowing more today and there is a chill in the air. Oh, I have on my bathing suit on, was hoping to get in the water, but my body is covered with chill bumps instead. I often feel a spray of water against my face as some waves crash against the shore. All around me are people, sea gulls, and pigeons; each just wondering around the beach not even aware of my presence. The birds walk a little closer to see if I have any food but none is to be found.

As I look across the horizon, I see several sail boats taking advantage of the wind. There are several charter fishing boats taking advantage of the sunshine and fishing opportunities of those visiting the area. Several people walk down the beach but are oblivious to me. Overhead a small plane flies enjoying the beautiful day. No one seems to care that I am alone.

The waves today are larger than they have been for the last couple of days; I guess as the wind blows harder the waves increase in size. Waves just fascinate me as they just continue to come and go over and over crashing against the shore in a never ending roar. I never really knew how noisy the ocean is until I experienced it a few years ago while visiting in the area and we would leave the door open all day and night. Sometimes we had to close it at night because we could not sleep because of the noise.

Jeremiah 31:35 says, *"Thus says the Lord, who gives the sun for light by day and the fixed order of the moon and the stars for light by night, who stirs up the sea so that its waves roar; "The Lord of Hosts is His name."* (NASB)

As I listen closely, I can even hear those words proclaimed, *"...The Lord of Hosts is His name."*

Some waves begin their cry off shore and then others just in the nick of time before they crash against the beach. They all join in the chorus they are to proclaim. It's a never ending shout of Praise to the Lord who created them to do just what they do. They don't seem to mind their calling. Even when they crash against the shore they quickly return to the ocean for more. Over and over they roar to the top of their voices, *"The Lord of Host is His name".*

What about you and me? Are we willing to do what God created us to do? Are we willing to continue again and again regardless if we are big or small? Are we willing to continue in our plot of life regardless of the pain we may feel when we're crashed into the beach, so to speak? Are we willing to follow through with our calling on the earth?

It is not always easy, but whenever we look at the ocean of

life, today is only a small part in which we play. Today is only a small period of time in comparison to eternity. Just like the waves that crash over and over, we need to be faithful again and again. God is always faithful. He never stops or gets tired of helping us even though, at times, we grow weary and tired. He is always there just waiting for us to call out for help.

Today as I sit here and enjoy the waves, God wants me to allow others to enjoy Him through me. In order to fulfill my calling, I must be open and honest while following His lead. Just as the waves of the ocean, I too need to continue my plight in life.

"Oh Father, Help us to not get bogged down in the hum drum of today and help us be faithful to praise you just like the waves of the ocean do. In Jesus Name, A-men."

Dying Produces Fruit

Have you ever questioned what you are here for? Have you ever wondered why God would choose you to be one of His children? Have you ever wondered why it seems that those who do not follow Christ seem to have more money, better careers, bigger house, cars, etc.?

This morning I read John 12: 20-26. Here we find that some Greeks were going to worship and they came to Phillip and told him they wanted to see Jesus. This event is happening just after the triumphal entry into Jerusalem just before Jesus' crucifixion. When Phillip came and told Jesus they wanted to see Him, Jesus explained that the hour had come for Him to be glorified. Then Jesus makes this statement in verse 24-26: *"Truly, truly, I say to you, unless a grain of wheat falls into the earth and dies, it remains alone; but if it dies, it bears much fruit He who loves his life loses it, and he who hates his life in this world will keep it to life eternal. If anyone serves Me, he must follow Me; and where I am, there My servant will be also; if anyone serves Me, the Father will honor him."* (NASB)

So what was Jesus trying to tell us? As we know, when you bury a seed into the ground it dies to what it currently is and goes through a changing process. When the seed dies, the outside shell pops open and behold, a little sprout pops out. The sprout then moves up toward the top of the soil and pops out of the ground. As it begins to grow and mature, in the spring, blooms will form and they eventually turn into fruit and provide nourishment for those who partake it.

Knowing all this, just what was Jesus meaning when He explains this process to his followers. Paul tells us, when we accept Jesus as our Savoir, "...*old things pass away and all things become new.*" (2 Corinthians 5:17b) This describes the dying process that takes place in our life.

I remember the day I gave my life to Christ like it was yesterday. As this process began in me; my language changed, my friends changed, my goals and desires changed. I was no longer content being the same person I was before. I had to die to who I had been for 31 years and allow Christ to change me.

If we look at the disciple's life, we can also see these same events take place. I guess Paul's life is really the most profound in that he went from persecuting Christians to being persecuted himself for the same thing. I would certainly classify that as a dying to self. If you look at Philippians 3: 4-6, we find the qualifications Paul had in his flesh to be God's child; "...*circumcised the eighth day, of the nation of Israel, of the tribe of Benjamin, a Hebrew of Hebrews, a Pharisee, as to zeal , a persecutor of the church; as to the righteousness which is in the Law, found blameless.*" (NASB) Paul was qualified in his flesh completely to be a follower of God, but notice he says in verse 7, *"But whatever things were gain to me, those things I have counted as loss for the sake of Christ."* (NASB) Following Christ became Paul's primary desire, no matter what the flesh represented it meant nothing to him.

So what benefit does it serve for us to die to our self? Well, Jesus said we will produce more fruit. So what does that mean? When we give our life to Jesus and begin to die to our self, our perspectives on life change. We begin to rejoice when things are hard. We pray without ceasing. Our life begins to touch others as they see us going through things differently than what most people do. In 2005, I lost my husband to a massive heart attack. Several people who worked with me asked me how I could handle it so well. This began to open doors for me to share with them that Jesus was carrying me. He had a plan for my life and I just needed to trust Him. I had the opportunity to share with one lady who prayed to accept Jesus as her Savior. As a result of all I went through I was able to produce fruit, fruit that will remain.

Many days, I wanted to just stay in bed, not go to work and be depressed. But God gave me the strength to not do it my way but do it His way. It was not easy but it was worth it all and today I have a whole new life.

So will this all be worth it in the end? In verse 26 of John 12, Jesus said, *"If anyone serves Me, he must follow Me; and where I am, there My servant will be also; if anyone serves Me, the Father will honor him."* (NASB) Yes, to be with Jesus where He is, will be worth it all. Does dying to self require us to give up some things here on this earth? Yes! We just have to remember that a mansion is being built, not with human hands but with God's own hand and it will give us the motivation to die to our self. I do not know about you but from what I have read about heaven it will definitely be worth it in the end.

You may be thinking, but what if the Bible is wrong and heaven is not real? Well, I have to tell you, I would rather come to the end of my life believing that there is a heaven and that everything we are told in the Bible is true than to have chosen to not believe it and in the end find out it was and then be cast into Hell with Satan and all his demons! What about you? Are you willing to die to yourself in order to produce fruit for Jesus? I sure hope so!

"Oh Father, help us to learn how to die to our self so You can use us to produce fruit that will remain. Help us to be willing to say, 'Here I am Lord, show me how to die in order to become all You want me to be. In Jesus Name, A-Men."

Is God AWOL?

During the first year of widowhood, God showed me many things. One thing I discovered was that He had not left me. Yes, He took my mate, my companion, my lover and friend, but God had not gone anywhere.

Do you ever feel like God is AWOL? Do you ever feel that just maybe God has forgotten you and left you all alone? Listen to what David, the man after God's own heart, says in Psalms 77:1-20

I yell out to my God, I yell with all my might,

I yell at the top of my lungs. He listens.

I found myself in trouble and went looking for my Lord.

My life was an open wound that wouldn't heal.

When friends said, "Everything will turn out all right."

I didn't believe a word they said.

I remember God—and shake my head.

I bow my head—then wring my hands.

I'm awake all night—not a wink of sleep;

I can't even say what's bothering me.

I go over the days one by one,

I ponder the years gone by.

I strum my lite all through the night,

Wondering how to get my life together.

Will the Lord walk off and leave us for good?

Will He never smile again?

Is His love worn threadbare?

Has his salvation promise burned out?

"Just my luck," I said. "The High God goes out of business just the moment I need him.

Once again I'll go over what God had done,

Lay out on the table the ancient wonders;

I'll ponder all the thing You've accomplished,

and give a long, loving look at your acts.

Oh God! Your way is holy!

No god is great like God!

You're the God who makes things happen; you showed everyone what you can do—

You pulled your people out of the worst kind of trouble,

Rescued the children of Jacob and Joseph.

Ocean saw You in action, God

Saw You and trembled with fear;

The deeps also trembled.

The clouds poured out water;

The skies gave forth a sound;

Your arrows flashed here and there.

The sound of Your thunder was in the whirlwind;

The lightings lit up the world;

The earth trembled and shook.

Your way was in the sea and Your paths in the mighty waters,

And your footprints may not be known.

You led Your people like a flock by the hand of Moses and Aaron.
(The Message)

So what do we learn from David when we are feeling like God has gone AWOL? We need to reflect back on the past and how God has brought us through. When we ponder the past we see multiple prayers answered, multiple times when our needs were met, many moments in time that God has brought people into our lives just at the right moment to help us. Then most of all we recall the fact that God is the same, yesterday, today and forever. He has not moved. He has not deserted us nor will He ever.

We do not always understand exactly what is going on or why things happen the way they do; but one thing we can do is trust that He is in control and He sees our needs and knows exactly what He is doing.

Since the death of my husband I have been able to look back and see God's hand moving in my life. I did not know for over a year what His plans for my future were but now I see things He had planned. I have begun a new life with another God fearing man and have experienced things that I never thought would have been possible. No, it has not been easy! Yes there have been times that I thought maybe I messed up but God has been faithful and is beginning to change me even more and allow me to see that He has a great future for our life together. I have learned that God is worthy of my trust, my reliance and His plan will be exactly what He wants. We just need to stop, listen, and walk as He tells us to do.

So when you think God has abandoned you, or feel that He may just have gone AWOL, ponder the past. Remember the times He has been there before and know that He DOES NOT CHANGE! He has not moved. Ask if there is something blocking your view, like unconfessed sin or just a season of stillness and then wait on

Him. Before you know it the Son will shine in your life again and then you will wonder why you ever doubted His love for you!

Ponder! Ponder! Ponder! This is the key!

"Oh Father, help us to remember that You never leave us. Help us remember that You are always there and that we just need to wait on You. Help us to not allow our emotions to get the most of us but to allow You to lead us into all truth. Help us to ponder the truth you have taken us through in the past and to remember that Your plan for our life is the perfect plan. In Jesus Name, A-Men."

Breaks in Our Cloudy Days

One cloudy and rainy day, as I was driving to work, I looked and suddenly there was a break in the clouds and the sun came shining through. I could see the blue sky behind the clouds and I began to thank the Lord for the brief view of the sun on an otherwise dreary day.

Then I remembered a plane ride I had taken several years before. As we were loading the plane, the clouds looked dark and mean. Rain was coming down hard and I began to get a little anxious. I wondered how the pilot would be able to see once we got up into the air; so I began to pray for safety. Once the plane took off, much to my amazement, we began to fly right through the clouds and viola, beautiful, clear blue sky! The clouds no longer looked dark and mean but beautiful, soft, white, and fluffy. It looked like you could just step out of the plane and float from one pillow to the other.

What an amazing transformation took place in my mind as I went from scared and a little fearful, to total peace, safe and felt secure. You know, that is how God is. Here in the world of mass confusion, troubles, trials, death, fears, anger, bitterness, hatred, killing, lying, cheating, etc., etc., etc... We sometimes wonder what in the world will happen next.

As we begin to reach up for help, as we call out to our Heavenly Father. He is right there. He sees our life from the top side. He knows the trial we are facing. He knows the problems in our life. He knows the challenges we face, and yet, He is right there waiting for us to just cry out for help, to reach out to Him. He is truly our ever present help in times of trouble.

Psalms 71:19-21 says, *"For Your righteousness, O God, reaches to the heavens, You who have done great things; O God, who is like You? You who have shown me many troubles and distresses will revive me again, and will bring me up again from the depths of the earth. May You increase my greatness and turn to comfort me."* (NASB)

Another scripture that comes to mind is Isaiah 54:10 which says, *"'For the mountains may be removed and the hills may shake, but My lovingkindness will not be removed from you, and My covenant of peace will not be shaken.' Says the Lord who has compassion on you."* (NASB)

One more, Isaiah 40:31, *"Yet those who wait for the Lord will gain new strength. They will mount up with wings like eagles, they will run and not get tired. They will walk and not become weary."* (NASB)

Many times in our life we become fearful of things which we have no need to be fearful about. We have worries about situations that we have no business worrying about. God is in control. He wants us to come up higher with Him. He wants us to soar with the eagles above the storms of life and allow Him to fix our problems.

So whenever you feel like the world is dark and dreary or that problems will crush you before the day is over, take a little break and remember that God is the sunshine above the clouds you may not see. He is all you need. He will break away the clouds of the day and allow the sun to brighten your day. All you have to do is take the time to reach up and allow Him to bring you up above the day and sit you on top of the problems. It is not nearly as bad when you see things from above the problems.

"Oh Lord, help us to reach up on our dreary days and allow Your sunshine to brighten our day. May You remind us to reach up whenever we get down and allow You to lift us up above the situation we face and see the pillows you have for us to lay on. Help us to just trust You and know that You are there waiting on us to release the problem in your hand and then allow us to fly above the cloud into the sunshine of Your Love. In Jesus Name, A-men."

Deborah Andre

Cool Days with a Little Rain

Yesterday as I was driving through town, I noticed that the leaves are beginning to turn and I see the first sign of fall upon me. I saw several trees that were just beautiful with their green, yellow and red colors. As I begin to think about when they started turning, I was reminded that over the last several weeks there has been some much cooler weather along with some rain.

As I pondered this I wondered, after having some cool days and a little rain in our life, do our colors shine as bright as these leaves did yesterday. Many times we experience dark gloomy days in our Spiritual life and we get discouraged and depressed. But you know, without those dark days we would not experience growth and change.

James 1:2-4 helps us to understand. It says, *"Consider it a sheer gift, friends, when test and challenges come at you from all sides. You know that under pressure, your faith-life is forced into the open and shows its true colors. So do not try to get out of anything prematurely. Let it do its work so you become mature*

30

and well-developed, not deficient in any way." (The Message)

As God takes us through those dark depressing days and patience is worked in us we become perfect and complete lacking in nothing. God takes our obedience to Him and accomplishes His perfect will.

I challenge you; if you are going through some dark days, look up! The Father is there and He wants you to spread around color that is beautiful to Him and to others. Reach up! He says, *"Cast your cares upon Me, Lay all your burdens at My feet, for My yoke is easy and My burden is light!"* Things will change and your true colors will shine!

"Thank you Lord that You do care for us and that You want to use us to spread around colors of Your love in this dark and dreary world. Help us to not run from what You are trying to perfect in our lives. Help Your colors in our life to shine through so others will see Jesus in the way we live. In Jesus Names, A-men."

Are You Really Changed?

This morning as I ponder what to write about, I ran across these words from Paul:

*"Since then, you have been raised with Christ, **set your heart on things above**, where Christ is seated at the right hand of God. Set you mind on things above, not on earthly things; for you died, and your life is now hidden with Christ in God. When Christ who is your life, appears, then you will also appear with Him in glory.*

*Put to death, therefore, whatever belongs to your earthy nature: sexual immorality, impurity, lust, evil desires and greed, which is idolatry. **Because of these, the wrath of God is coming.** You used to walk in these ways, in the life you once lived. But how **you must rid yourselves** of all such things as these; anger, rage, malice, slander, filthy language from your lips. Do not lie to each other, since you have taken off your old self with its practices and have put on the new self, which is being renewed in knowledge in the image of its Creator. Where there is no Greek or Jew, circumcised or uncircumcised, barbarian,*

Scythian, slave or free, but Christ is all, and is in all.

*Therefore, as **God's chosen people**, holy and dearly loved, **clothe yourselves with compassion, kindness, humility, gentleness and patience. Bear with each other and forgive whatever grievances you may have against one another.** Forgive as the Lord forgave you. And over all these virtues put on love, which binds them all together in perfect unity."* (Colossians 3:1-14 (NIV); Emphasis Mine.)

This scripture is very plain about what we, as Christians, are to do. Once we accept Christ as our Savior and Lord we are no longer free to stay the same way as we were. We are dead to our old life, therefore, we are to be different. Many times we do not understand how to do these new things. Jesus sent the Holy Spirit to live in our hearts and He is responsible to lead and guide us into all truth.

So what do we have to do in order to walk in love and clothe ourselves with compassion, kindness, humility, gentleness and patience? We must call on the name of the Lord to help us and show us where we are failing in these areas. God wants to give us these things but we must be willing to change and turn away from the fleshly nature.

Are you willing to do that? I hope so, because then and only then will we be able to hear our Father say, "Well done, my good and faithful servant!"

"Oh Father, help us to walk away from the fleshly nature we are given. Help us to walk in the Spirit and display His characteristics. Lord, without Your help there is no way we can do this. Please help us! In Jesus Name, A-men"

Suffering for Righteousness

Have you ever been gossiped about? Have you ever had a time when you knew that you did nothing wrong but people in your world thought differently and they talked about you and spread vicious rumors about you?

This morning in my quiet time, I began to read in 1 Peter 3:13-22 and found some encouraging words I want to share with you. Peter is telling us that it really does not matter what others say about you. What matters is what Christ says about you.

"Who is there to harm you if you prove zealous for what is good? But even if you should suffer for the sake of righteousness, you are blessed. And do not fear their intimidation and do not be troubled. But sanctify Christ as Lord in your hearts, always being ready to make a defense to everyone who asks you to give an account for the hope that is in you, yet with gentleness and reverence; and keep a good conscience so that in the thing in which you are slandered, those who revile your good behavior in Christ will be put to shame." (1Peter 3:13-16 NASB)

This says to me that the battle is not mine but it is the Lord's. As long as I am doing what I am supposed to do then I do not need to worry about what others are saying about me. I just need to keep myself pure before Christ because that is all that matters.

Many years ago, God taught me that I am only accountable to Him for myself. I am not accountable for anyone else. So no matter what others say or think, I need to just keep my mouth shut and stay in touch with the Master. I need to make sure I am not caught up in all the gossip and pull myself down to the level of the other person.

Satan loves it whenever he uses people to accomplish his will and then pulls those of us who are right with Christ into the middle of all his devouring and tearing others apart.

My challenge to you today is to not get upset when others are talking about you and certainly do not allow yourself to be pulled down to their level, just remember this: *"For it is better, if God should will it so, that you suffer for doing what is right rather than for doing what is wrong."* (1 Peter 3:17)

Oh Father, help me to remember that the only thing that matters is what you think of me. No matter what others may say or think, You are the only one I answer to. Help me to just keep my thoughts pure, my heart in tune with you and my mouth shut, In Jesus Name I pray. A-men"

Clean Hands and a Pure Heart

In 2005, the "See You at the Pole" theme was "Ascend". The verse they used was Psalms 24:4-5 which says, *"Who may ascend to the hill of the Lord? Who may stand in His holy place? He who has clean hands and a pure heart..."*(NASB) Wow! What a challenge for us today.

I believe many in our world today are being trapped by sin and the consequences of not turning from them. Because of our entrapment we cannot ascend the hill of the Lord because we do not have clean hands and a pure heart.

It is now time for Christians to take a stand in our country. We need to "come out of the closet" and stop allowing our rights to be removed. It is time that we fall on our face and confess our sins and ask God to help us in overcoming the entrapment that we are experiencing in our country of political correctness. It is time for us to truly worship God the way David did.

As you look at our world we see more and more evil, I know that the Bible tells us that things are just going to get worse and worse, but I, for one, want to continue to experience God's presence in my daily life and want to be found pleasing to Him.

We as a nation need to remember that God was involved in the forming of our country and the freedoms that we experience are a product of people crying out to Him for freedom. I pray that we will begin to heed the verse that says,

*"**If** my people, who are called by My name, **will humble** themselves and **pray** and **seek** my face and **turn** from their wicked ways, **then** I will hear from heaven and will **forgive** their sins and will **heal** their land."* (2 Chronicles 7:14 NASB, emphasis mine)

This verse came to Solomon after he dedicated the temple to the Lord and has prayed and asked God to come and rest in the temple. After anointing the temple with many sacrifices and the Israelites kneeling on their faces worshipping God and saying, *"He is good; His love endures forever."* That night God appeared to Solomon and told him that He had heard the prayer and chosen this place for Himself as a temple. He then said that when He shut up the heavens and there was no rain or commanded locusts to devour the land or send a plague among my people that if they would call on Him and turn, then He would hear them and heal their land.

We are God's temple today. In our land we see forest fires, floods, freezes like we have never seen before, as well as devastating hurricanes. He has chosen us for His dwelling place. It is time for us to bow our knee before Him, confess our sins, turn from our wicked ways in order to have before Him clean hands and a pure heart; then we can ask that our land be healed.

"Oh Lord, help us walk in obedience to You today. Convict us of our sins so we can confess them. Help us have clean hands and a pure heart before Your presence. Use us, Oh Lord, as we seek Your Face. In Jesus Name, A-men."

Repent, Believe and Trust

While driving in my car, listening to the book of Acts, several things caught my attention. In Acts 8:14-23 Peter and John are in Samaria because of all the people there being saved. Peter questioned if they had received the Holy Spirit and they told them they had not heard of Him. So Peter and John prayed for them and began laying their hands on them, and they received the Holy Spirit.

The thing that really caught my attention was a man by the name of Simon who was there watching these events take place. He approached Peter and John and offered them money and said, *"Give this authority to me as well; so that everyone on whom I lay my hands may receive the Holy Spirit."* Peter couldn't believe his ears, this man actually wanted to buy the gift of God? Peter then hold him to repent of this wickedness and pray for the intention of his heart to be changed. Of course Simon refused to do this, in fact, he told Peter to pray for him so that nothing he had spoken would happen to him.

As I pondered this event, I thought about all the people in our world today who are guilty of this very thing. They watch TV evangelist who encouraged them to send them money for "prayer clothes", "special oil", "pieces of material", etc. in order to be blessed by God, double their money, have their bills paid, etc. Even on Facebook or in our e-mail accounts we are told to forward this message to 5 or 10 other people in the next 5 minutes so we will be granted our wish or to prevent bad things from happening to us. How foolish we are to believe all this stuff.

God does not need our money, He cannot be bought! God just wants us to repent, believe, and walk in obedience to Him. If we trust Him with all our heart He will direct our path and give us the desires of our heart. We should not ever think that we can buy His blessings or anything that He has to offer. If this could be done then Jesus would not have even had to come to die for our sins. We are only helping these people get rich.

So do you trust God? Are you trying to buy His blessings? Repent, knowing that He loves you and just wants us to repent, believe and trust in His Holy Name.

"Oh Father, I pray you will show us what we need to do in order to receive Your blessings. Help us to trust You and You alone. Help us to walk in obedience, allow You to change our hearts and give us strength to become all You want us to be. In Jesus Name, A-men."

For Such a Time as This

"*...For God sent me before you to preserve life.*" (Genesis 45:5B NASB.)

This is the statement Joseph made when he revealed his identity to his brothers. They had returned to the palace after being framed for stealing his drinking cup. If you know the story, you know that Joseph's brothers had hated him as a child and had sold him into slavery. After arriving in Egypt, the caravan who had bought him sold him to Pharaoh to be a household servant. God was with Joseph and blessed everything he did. However, Joseph experienced many trials and was even thrown into prison for a crime he never committed. God continued to bless Joseph because of his obedience to Him and at this time he was in control of all the grain in Egypt during a famine that was in the land. God had prepared Joseph for this famine and he was selling grain to other countries because the famine was great in all the land. Joseph's father heard that this was happening in Egypt so he sent his son's to buy grain to feed their family.

Joseph recognized his brother's; however, the brothers did not recognize him. He tricked them by returning their money for the grain and then having them brought back to him accusing them of stealing. He was planning to keep one of the brothers while they went back to Canaan. They begged Joseph to not send them home without their brother because it would kill their father with grief. As Joseph's heart was touched by their concern for their father, he revealed himself to them. Joseph realized that God had sent him to Egypt in order to be in his position to save his family.

Joseph was a godly man. He had endured many trials in order to get to where he was now and it was all revealed at this time. God's plan was to spare the Israelites and because of Joseph's obedience, the plan was carried out. Never once in scripture do we see Joseph complain about all he was going through. Never once does it say he doubted God was in control. We only see his obedience no matter the situation he found himself in.

I wonder how many times in our life we go through trials and situations so that God can use us for a particular reason. Over and over in scripture we see events take place and people have been put into positions to accomplish God's will and preserve life. Esther was told that she was a queen "for such a time as this."

If we are unhappy with the situation we find our self in, maybe we need to stop and ask God if we are where we are for such a time as this. God has a plan for each of us and He knows the situation we are in and He wants to use us to accomplish His will. So ask Him to reveal His plan to you, then open your eyes and look. You may be surprised at what you find.

"Oh Father, Help us to realize that we are where we are because of You and what You have planned. Help us to realize that we are in this place for such a time as this. Show us Your will and help us to accomplish whatever it is You have planned. In Jesus Name, A-men."

God Cares about the Little Things

Have you ever wondered if God really cared about the little things in your life or even if you should pray about these things? I have had people come to me about what seemed to them as insignificant problem. My first question to them is, "Have you prayed about it?" They are so surprised that I would even suggest that God cares about this little situation. Their response is that they do not want to bother God with it because it was just a little thing. They then confess that they only pray about the major decisions in their life. They handle the little things themselves but then a problem comes up in that situation and now they are frustrated and don't know what to do.

As you read the scripture in Exodus where God is giving Moses the instructions about how to build the tabernacle, the breastplate, the ephod and the other things to be used in worshipping Him, He goes into every little detail about each piece. As I pondered this, I realize that God does care about the little things. God even told him exactly where to put the rings for the curtain rods for the tabernacle, exactly what type of stones to use in the breastplate, exactly how big they were to be and in which order to place them on the garment. God is very specific about all the instructions and scripture tells us that they did everything exactly as the Lord commanded Moses.

If God cares this much about the details of the tabernacle, then He cares about every detail of our lives. We are His children; we are the tabernacle of today, so why wouldn't He care? Sometimes if I am looking for a pair of earrings in my jewelry box and am unable to find them, I ask quickly for His help in finding them and they will pop up to the top of the box. This may sound silly but it is true. God does not want us to do anything without asking Him that's why we are told to *"Pray without ceasing."* We are to be in a continual attitude of prayer asking Him for everything we need. I have prayed about parking spots in the mall, about finding the perfect dress for the least amount of money, etc. And guess what, He did it!

Here is a quick example. When Shelby and I got married we decided on a Monday to have the wedding on Saturday. We knew God was in it and that this was exactly what He wanted to happen. He had confirmed this to us over and over. So I called my sister and asked her to order us a cake. I went to buy a dress, told the Lord that He knew I didn't have much money so I needed a nice dress for a little money. I went into David's Bridal Shop and found a $200 dress on sale for $60. It fit perfect and looked great; went down the street to Garden Ridge to get some flowers for my bouquet. I looked and looked, then said a quick prayer, walked over to the bridal flower area and there it was, a bouquet of calla lilies already made up for $20.00. My pastor was going to be out of town on Saturday and could not marry us so I talked with the chaplain at the hospital where I worked and he agreed to do the ceremony.

Saturday morning we went to the church to decorate a unity candle table. We used some flowers and cloth that my niece had used in her wedding. It was perfect. Then when we went to pick up the cake, guess what? The exact flowers and colors we had used to decorate the unity candle table was exactly what the lady had put on my cake! You call that coincidence? Not me, I say that God cared about the details of our wedding. My niece even gave us a song for the wedding, "God Blessed the Broken Road" which was perfect for our situation. The words of that song completely expressed the thoughts of our heart that day. God did bless us and He did put us together to accomplish His will for our life.

So my challenge to you is to realize that God cares about the little things. Even if you feel that it is unimportant, God doesn't. Take it to Him and ask for His guidance in everything about your life. Only He can lead you in the right way.

"Oh Father, Help us realize that You do care about the little things in our lives. Help us take everything to You in prayer and seek Your face in all that we do. Show us what You would have us do and give us wisdom to follow Your leadership continually. In Jesus Name, A-men."

Worrying about Tomorrow

I do not know about you but time is flying by for me. I do not have a clue where the last seven years have gone but they are. I remember a scripture in Matthew 6:33-34 where Jesus tells the disciples *"For this reason I say to you, do not be worried about your life, as to what you will eat or what you will drink; nor for your body, as to what you will put on. Is not life more than food, and the body more than clothing? Look at the birds of the air, that they do not sow, nor reap nor gather into barns, and yet your heavenly Father feeds them. Are you not worth much more than they? And who of you by being worried can add a single hour to his life?"* (Matt. 6:25-27 NASB) He then tells them in verse 33-34; *"Seek first His kingdom and His righteousness, and all these things will be added to you. So do not worry about tomorrow; for tomorrow will care about itself. Each day has enough trouble of its own."* (NASB)

Many times we worry about the tomorrow of our lives. We waste so much time worrying about things that may or may not happen. If we evaluate the time we spend worried over things that never really come to pass, I believe we would be shocked at how much time we have really wasted in a day. Jesus comforts us here and very plainly tells us not to worry about tomorrow.

Instead of worrying, we need to ask God to show us what He wants us to do for Him today. Tomorrow may not come and if we have spent the whole day worrying about it, we have really just wasted today.

My challenge for you is get busy doing today whatever God leads you to do for we do not have time to waste this day worrying about things that may or may not happen. And even if what we are worrying about does happen, what can we really do to change it? Nothing! God is in control and He alone can give us wisdom for today. Seek His Kingdom first and He will meet the needs for tomorrow.

"Oh Father, Help us not to worry but just trust in You Alone!"

God Has a Plan

God has a plan for your life and if you just trust and rely on Him, He will give you the desires of your heart.

This is a very hard statement to grab ahold of whenever your world has been turned upside down through the loss of a loved one, loss of a job, loss of financial security or some other tragedy you may find yourself in. I can testify to this truth when I found myself in the car with my husband having a massive heart attack and he left this world leaving me behind. We had just gotten to the place where we were happy with life. He had a job he loved, we were serving in a church we loved, we had our own place, and we were financially doing ok with the hope of a long life together. It was the week before our 30th wedding anniversary and we just knew that things were going to be good. Then it happened. My world came crashing down.

Over the next 11 months I experienced anger at my husband for leaving me, hurt from people who had been in my life for 30 plus years that I thought loved me, rejection by other people I called friends, and then love for those who truly were my family and friends.

As I struggled with what God was up to and what His

plans were I found this scripture: 2 Chronicles 16:9; *"For the eyes of the Lord move to and fro throughout the earth that He may strongly support those whose heart is completely His..."* Yes, I made some mistakes along the healing process. I experienced great anger, distress, rejection, lack of wisdom in some decisions I made but all the time the Lord was right there waiting for me to turn back to Him.

As I attended a funeral 11 months after my devastating crisis and the message was completely for me. The message was from Jeremiah 29:11-13 which says, *"'for I know the plans that I have for you,' declares the Lord, 'plans for welfare and not for calamity to give you a future and a hope. Then you will call upon Me and come and pray to Me, and I will listen to you. You will seek Me and find Me when you search for Me with all your heart.'"*

That day as I drove back home, I went to the cemetery, yelled and screamed at my husband whose body was in that grave and then I sat down on the wall beside the grave and cried until I could not cry any more. I prayed and asked God to forgive me for the anger I had had and asked Him to heal my heart and my soul. And He did.

Over the next several months I spent a lot of time on my knees, seeking His face and the plans He had for my life. After all, I am living today only because of Him and only for His plan. God knew everything about me. He looks at the whole picture of my life that He planned out. I just had to learn to trust Him, believe

His word and take all the bad thoughts Satan used against me
captive to the obedience of Christ.

I read this poem "The Weaving" by Corrie Ten Boone and
I believe it is the true for all our lives. It says:

"My life is but a weaving

Between my Lord and me.

I cannot choose the colors

He worketh steadily.

Oftimes He weaveth sorrow,

And I in foolish pride

Forget He sees the upper

And I the underside.

Not 'til the loom is silent

And the shutters cease to fly

Shall God unroll the canvas

And explain the reason why.

The dark threads are as needful

In the weaver's skillful hand

As the threads of gold and silver

In the pattern He has planned.

"Oh Father, Help me and those reading this understand that You are working a beautiful plan for our lives. Help us to be willing to accept the hard times as You work them out for our good. Help us to trust You to know what is best and help us accept the dark threads as much as those of gold and silver, In Jesus Name. A-men."

Direction for Your Paths

"Trust in the Lord with all your heart, lean not on your own understanding, in all your ways acknowledge Him and He will direct your paths." Proverbs 3:5-6

Have you ever wondered if this is really true? Have you ever just trusted God and not try to figure things out. Well, this is exactly what I did after I fell on my knees and gave God my life.

After the realization of my husband's death, I began to really seek God for what He wanted from me. I told Him if being alone was what He had for me to do then it was fine. But if He had someone out there to just "drop him out of the sky and show me he was the one". The next morning I received an e-mail card from a man in South LA who was on the same internet singles site as I was. Amazingly enough God blessed me with a man who loved Him as much as I do, who had lost his wife of 36 years to cancer and was also seeking God for someone to share his life with.

As we began to communicate, meet, and shared our dreams and desires with each other, it became apparent to us both that God was in the middle of it all. After only 27 days we married. People thought we were nuts. My children about had a stroke and the people in the church he pastored spread vicious rumors about us but God gave us complete peace in the midst of it all.

It has now been 7 years and we have both been amazed at how God has worked in our lives. Has it always been easy? No. Has everything gone according to what we had planned? No. But has God given us direction along the way? Absolutely!

We have grown so much in our relationship. We have learned more and more about each other and are open and honest about all that we need and do. We are free to talk about our spouses who have gone before us and frequent the cemeteries to place flowers on each grave.

All of our children have accepted our lives and we are becoming a real family. It is amazing how God is directing and leading us as we seek His face.

If you had told us 8 years ago this would have happened we would both have probably laughed out loud; but God has proven He can be trusted. He will direct our paths. We may not understand all that has happened or will happen in the future but we know that He is directing everything in our path.

So, do not try and figure it all out! You may never really understand why or how but as we acknowledge Him, He will direct our paths. Just believe His word because it will never fail you!

"Oh Father, help us to truly trust You! Help us to really lean not on our own understanding because we just get confused, worry, stress and many times lose hope. Help us to just trust You and give You our paths in this life. Direct us as only You can and show us Your plans because we know that only then will we have the peace that passes all understanding You alone give. In Jesus name, A-men."

God: Loving and Just

A few years ago I did a study of the Minor Prophets. I did an extensive study in the book of Nahum and found some interesting truths about the God we serve. Nahum had a vision that was addressed to Nineveh but I believe it is applicable for today also.

In the first chapter, Nahum describes the God which we serve. Many people in our world today believe that God is just a loving God. And it is true, He loves but He is also a God of justice for those who come against Him. In Nahum 1:2-3 we see the following:

"A jealous and avenging God is the Lord; The Lord is avenging and wrathful. The Lord takes vengeance on His adversaries, and He reserves wrath for His enemies. The Lord is slow to anger and great in power and the Lord will by no means leave the guilty unpunished. In whirlwind and storm is His way, and clouds are the dust beneath His feet."(NASB)

This verse can be looked at two ways. It should be scary for those who are coming against our God and His people. They should be fearful to read who they are messing with.

Verse 1:7 says, *"The Lord is good, A stronghold in the day of trouble and He knows those who take refuge in Him."* (NASB) This is comforting for those of us who are on His side.

My question is this, will you face the avenging wrathful God one day or will you receive the goodness of God? I have pity for those who are against God because one day they will answer to Him. One day they will give an account for the evil they have done and the reasons that they have come against Him and His people .

As you study the Bible, the back of the book is plain. God wins and those who are on His side will win also. Unless your name is written in the Lamb's Book of Life you will be cast into hell with Satan and his angels. Remember, hell was not created for man, but many are choosing to go there because they reject the greatest gift ever given to the world. Jesus Christ came, born of a virgin, lived a perfect life, died on the cross for sins He never committed, rose again the third day and now offers everyone on the earth the free gift of salvation. Jesus told Nicodemus in John chapter 3 that we must be born again; this event is more than just believing in God but accepting His free gift and giving Him complete control of our lives.

I meet people every day that say they believe in God or they go to some church or are a part of some religion but this is not enough. James tells us that even Satan believes in God and trembles.

Jesus told His disciples before He left that He was going to prepare a mansion for them and that He would return and get them so that they may dwell where He is.

So, what about you? Heaven or Hell? Vengeance and wrath from a just God or a mansion built by His own hands? The choice is yours! As the Holy Spirit draws you, fall on your knees, confess your sins and ask Him to save you. One day you will not regret it.

"Oh Father, please draw us to You by the Holy Spirit. Help us to surrender our will to become all You would have us to be. Help us to seek Your face and allow You to have total control, In Jesus Name, A-men."

Goals for the Christian Life

As I studied 1 Thessalonians I found some very timely goals to live by. I don't know about you but I believe Jesus could come any minute and if you are like me, you only want to hear one thing, "Well done, my good and faithful servant!" As we study scripture, God gives us explicit instructions in order to be found spotless and blameless when He returns and this in only one set of those goals to live by.

In chapter 5 of 1 Thessalonians these can be found in verses 12-22. I have summed them up in a list for you.

- Appreciate those who diligently labor among you and have charge over you in the Lord and give instruction
- Esteem them very highly in love because of their work
- Live in peace with one another.
- Admonish the unruly.
- Encouraged the fainthearted.
- Help the weak.
- Be patient with everyone.
- See that no one repays another with evil for evil.

- Always seek after that which is good for one another and for all people.
- Rejoice always.
- Pray without ceasing
- In everything give thanks; for this is God's will for you in Christ Jesus
- Do not quench the Spirit
- Do not despise prophetic utterances.
- Examine everything carefully.
- Hold fast to that which is good.
- Abstain from every form of evil.

I am convinced that if all Christians will strive to do these things then we will be found being faithful to the calling on our life and many non-believers would listen to what we have to say and have a desire to have what we have. I believe this is why we are failing to see people's lives changed because we, as followers of Jesus, are not living in a way that is different than the world.

Many churches today are preaching to itchy ears. People do not want to hear the truth because it will cause them to give up things they hold on to, however, as we study the life of Paul and the example he left us this is exactly what we need to do. Paul's life was radically changed and so will we be if we just trust in God and allow Him to change us.

Remember this scripture, "...*He who began a good work in you will perfect it until the day of Christ Jesus.*" (Philippians 1:6b NASB)

"Oh Father, help us to begin to live our lives according to the instructions in Your word. Help us to be an example to those lost and dying in our world today. Help us to have the desire to serve You completely and fully. Help us in our daily walk until the day Jesus returns to take us home. In Jesus Name, A-men"

America in Lamentations

While studying the book of Lamentations, a picture of the USA keeps popping into my head. Lamentations is the crying of Jerusalem after they fell captive by their enemies and how it all happened. In America we have had a fall of the financial market and a cry of people who have lost their jobs and some have experienced losing everything they have worked for their whole life. One thing we need to remember is that when we put our faith and trust in anything this world has to offer we are making a very big mistake.

We are told in Lamentations that Jerusalem has just had a love affair with their enemies. Everything was going so well that they turned their backs on the Lord and His commands. Then when the enemies, once their lovers, took control and eventually took them into captivity it hits them, they turned their back on the Lord, stopped following His commands and begin to do things their own way. Whenever this happens, God turns His back, the blessings stop flowing and before you know it the enemy takes control.

I am amazed how in America we have forgotten why this country was established. Children today are being taught a different history concerning our country when in reality our founding fathers based this country on serving God, His word and following the Ten Commandments.

Is it really any surprise that our financial system has fallen, people are unable to pay their debt, kids are killing each other and their parents, suicide is up, drugs are rampant and everything appears to be falling apart?

One thing we need to remember, the Lord has not left us, we have walked away from Him. In Lamentations 1:18a, the writer says, *"The Lord is righteous; For I (Jerusalem) have rebelled against His command..."* (NASB) As you read on you see that Jerusalem begins to understand why things are falling apart. Why their lovers have become their enemies, their families are selling everything they have just to feed their families and their greatness is falling apart.

Here in America we see the same things happening. A couple years ago Ed McMan spoke of selling his precious possessions for gold during a Super Bowl ad. Today we see famous people falling into drugs, alcohol and ruining their lives for things that never satisfy. These who were once great are falling into this trap the enemy has set for America. There is no hope for America unless we turn back to the Lord.

Lamentations 3:22-33; 40-42 says, *"The Lord's loving kindnesses indeed never cease, for His compassions never fail. They are new every morning; Great is Your faithfulness. The Lord is my portion," says my soul, "therefore I have hope in Him." The Lord is good to those who wait for Him, to the person who seeks Him. It is good that he waits silently for the salvation of the Lord. It is good for a man that he should bear the yoke in his youth. Let him sit alone and be silent since he has laid it on him. Let him put his mouth in the dust, perhaps there is hope. Let him give his cheek to the smiter, Let him be filled with reproach. For the Lord will not reject forever, for if He causes grief, then He will have compassion according to His abundant lovingkindness. For He does not afflict willingly or grieve the sons of men...Let us examine and probe our ways, and let us return to the Lord. We lift up our hearts and hands toward God in heaven; we have transgressed and rebelled, You have not pardoned. "* (NASB)

The lament continues to cry out to God and ask for mercy. I am reminded of the passage in 2 Chronicles 7:12-15, *"Then the Lord appeared to Solomon at night and said to him, 'I have heard your prayer and have chosen this place for Myself as a house of sacrifice. If I shut up the heavens so that there is no rain, or if I command the locust to devour the land, or if I send pestilence among My people, and my people who are called by My name humble themselves and pray and seek My face and turn from their wicked ways, then I will hear from heaven, will forgive their sins and will heal their land. Now My eyes will be open and My ears attentive to the prayer offered in his place. '"* (NASB)

This friend is the answer to our problems. We must turn back to the Lord. We must turn from our sins and ask the Lord for His mercy on our lives and our country, and then He will hear our cry and save us and heal our land.

What about you? Have you turned your back on the Lord and allowed the enemy to become your lover? Have you said to yourself, "it really does not matter what I do? It really does not matter what God says in His word, I can do things the way I want to and it will be ok?"

We need to learn what Jerusalem learned, nothing is hidden from God, He sees it all and when we begin to do things our way and turn from His way, He will turn His back and everything will begin to fall apart. We are only hurting ourselves and grieving His heart because it does matter to Him. If we are His children, we will not get away from accepting sin and even encouraging it. We will not be OK until we turn back to Him and allow His Spirit to lead us.

Now is the time to turn around, repent, confess your sins and turn back to God so that He can restore you and plant you once again by streams of living water. Why would we not want that? It is our answer for today. Whoever the president is or whoever is in the other offices of our government is not the answer to our problems. God is!

"Oh Father, help us to learn to read Your word and learn from it. Help us to bend our knee to You and allow You the freedom in our lives and our country. Help us to turn back to You, seek Your face and allow You to take control. Only then will we ever experience True Peace. In Jesus Name, A-men."

Full of His Glory

Many times in our world today we get caught up in listening to the news, reading the newspaper and suddenly we get depressed because of all that is going on in our world today and we begin to think everything is bad.

As you read God's word, the truth of the matter is revealed to us. In Isaiah 6: 1-3 we read Isaiah say, *"In the year of King Uzziah's death I saw the Lord sitting on a throne, lofty and exalted, with the train of His robe filling the temple. Seraphim stood above Him, each having six wings: with two he covered his face, and with two he covered his feet and with two he flew. And one called out to another and said, "Holy, Holy, Holy, is the Lord of host, the whole earth is full of His glory."*(NASB)

Did you see that last phrase? "The whole earth is full of His glory!" Then why are we so depressed and unable to see it? As I pondered this part of the scripture I went outside to watch the sunrise and listen to and watch the birds. As I sat there, I began to ask God to allow me to see His glory. As the sun came up above the horizon I could look at it until it became so bright my eyes had to look away. I asked God if that was a picture of His glory.

Then as I began to watch the birds as they flew above my head; it was brought to my attention the different sounds each species makes and as they fly, they each have a different wing pattern by which to travel. Some of them make quick flaps of their wings, while others slowly moved theirs and still others flap several times and then just soar. Amazing how they each are created to worship God is a different way.

As I pondered how different the birds are I was reminded that each of us are different also. We each have special gifts God has given to us, we have different features and yet we are all created in His image. As I pondered the fact that the whole earth is full of God's glory, I asked myself, why we are always looking at the faults of people, bad events and circumstances of our life. Even when the weathermen are giving the forecast for the day they always say there is a 40% chance of showers and yet in reality there is also a 60% chance of sunshine. Cloudy, rainy days cause people to get depressed so why not look at the good side of the weather so our spirits are uplifted and not depressed?

I believe that it is because Satan is the prince of this world and he wants us to be unhappy, depressed, and miserable and is always trying to rob us of the Glory of God. Remember, God told us that Satan roams around like a roaring lion, seeking who he can rip apart. And sadly enough we allow him to do just that.

I do not know about you, but I am ready to see the Glory of God fill the earth! I'm ready to reread the back of the book that tells us plainly that we win in the end. So no matter how bad things may look, no matter how bad you feel or how bad the weather is, look up for the Glory of the Lord fills the whole earth. Praise Him, Honor Him and Rejoice, our Redemption Draws near!

"Oh Father, I thank You that Your Glory does fill all the earth. Thank You that You never change. Thank You that we can trust You and allow You to fill us up with Your glory Every day!"

Covered with Feathers

Psalms 91: 1-4 says, *"He who dwells in the shelter of the Most High will abide in the shadow of the Almighty. I will say to the Lord, "My refuge and my fortress, My God, in whom I trust!" For it is He who delivers you from the snare of the trapper and from deadly pestilence. He will cover you with His pinions, and under His wings you may seek refuge. His faithfulness is a shield and bulwark."*(NASB)

As I read these first four verses of this Psalm I was reminded of a story I once heard of a woman who lived in Dallas. She stopped at a red light one day and a man jumped into her car with a knife. (This was before we had automatic door locks!) The man told her to drive where he told her to. She said she was so scared and remembered that there was a scripture in the Bible about God hiding us under His wings or something to that effect. She said, "I could not remember exactly how the scripture went however when we stopped at the next light I began to flap my arms and say, "feather's Lord, feathers, cover me with your feathers." She said that the man looked at her and said, "Woman you are crazy" and he jumped out of the car and ran.

We never know when we need something special from the

Lord but obviously, from this story, we are reminded of how important God's word should be to us as His children. We need to listen to Him. We need to hide His word in our heart so we don't sin against Him and then when a time comes and we need to be covered with His feathers we can remember the scripture and use it to defeat our enemies.

God loves you and He wants to lead you in the right path and then cover you when you get into situations you may not know how to handle. Obliviously this woman was covered and protected by His feathers and we are reminded that we can seek refuge in Him. Remember, whenever you need the Lord, just whisper a prayer and He will cover you with His feathers.

"Oh Father, I thank You so much that You do cover us with Your feathers. Thank You that You are all we need in our times of trouble and Your faithfulness is a shield and bulwark to us. Give us the desire to study Your word more. Give us the desire to put it to memory so that when we need it the Holy Spirit can cause us to be reminded of the truth You have given us. In Jesus Name, A-men."

God's Hand at Work

Summer has come and gone. Fall is here. Soon we will begin seeing the changing leaves in our area and the bareness of winter will not be far behind. I love the fall because of all the new colors that appear on the trees; red, yellow, orange, maroon as well as any combination of these colors.

These changes remind us how amazing our Father is. He has the ability to take a beautiful green tree and make it orange or red. It happens in a very short time frame and then those beautiful leaves drop to the ground and the tree are bear for the winter months. Before you know it the leaves will begin to bud again and the process starts all over. How can anyone really look at these events and say there is no God. Not only this process but a lot of other processes we see in our world that take place. Then people say, "There is no God! This just happened by chance". Really?

Psalms 135:1; 5-7 says this: *"Praise the Lord! Praise the name of the Lord; Praise Him, O servants of the Lord... For I know that the Lord is great and that our Lord is above all gods. Whatever the Lord pleases, He does, in heaven and in earth, in the seas and in all deeps. He causes the vapors to ascend from the ends of the earth; who makes lightning's for the rain, Who bring forth the wind from His treasuries."*(NASB)

So you see, Our God is in charge no matter what someone's opinion is, this fact remains; He controls the times, seasons, years, and all events that happen in our world today. It is all filtered through the hand of God. He is the one true God and He alone is worthy of our praise!

Joshua 21:45 reminds us; *"Not one of the good promises which the Lord had made to the house of Israel failed; all came to pass."*(NASB)

If God's promises came to pass then, they will continue to come to pass today. As Jesus told the disciples, He is preparing for us, His children, mansions in Heaven and I believe we will get to see it very soon. As you begin to see the changing leaves in the fall, remember that all those colors are just a glimpse into heaven for us and God is still in control of it all.

"Oh Father, I thank You for the beautiful colored leaves in the fall. I thank You for the refreshing time that takes place in the winter months and most of all I thank You for the new growth in the spring time. Thank You for reminding us You are in control and Your hand is always at work in and around us, we just need to look up! In Jesus Name, A-men."

Seasons in Our Christian Walk

I believe that just like the earth goes through its seasons of Spring, Summer, Fall and Winter, so do we in our Spiritual lives.

Spring and fall are my favorite times of the year. Spring because after the dead of winter everything is new, refreshed and green; fall because of the beautiful colors. I love seeing the trees as they slowly change from a deep green to muted reddish green then to a bright red. Some trees actually have three colors at one time. Some trees turn to bright yellow, others orange, others just go brown. Then one day, while driving down the same road, all the leaves are gone; mostly covering the ground underneath the trees and everything looks empty, dry and dead.

During the times of winter we have very cold and dreary days. The lush green foliage of summer has changed from beautiful colors to dark brown and it is now on the ground. Even some of the animals have hibernated into caves and settled into their nest. A lot of birds have flown south and there are no longer sweet melodies being made by them as you walk outside. Most of the time there is just silence except for the crunch of dead leaves under your feet as you walk through the yard or in the woods. Every now and then you may hear the sound of a barking squirrel but there is mostly silence.

As winter progresses and we are cold and feeling down, suddenly it snows and everything takes on a new appearance. The morning sky may be pink; the trees have white lined limbs and the ground is no longer looking dead but pure and clean with a white colored blanket. The air is now cold and crisp. Many times, after a beautiful snow, you can walk outside and experience total silence as the white blanket spreads over the earth.

When the snow is falling, I love to sit by the fireplace, hearing the wood as it crackles and pops while watching as everything turns white. As I look around I may see a red bird land on a snow covered limb of a tree, a glimmer of joy fills my heart as I remember when I was about 11 or 12 and I saw a red bird sitting on a limb and as I looked at the limbs around it they formed a perfect heart and the bird sat in the center. It is a beautiful memory in the mind of my childhood.

Often I wonder why we go through these "winter" times in our Christian lives. Some people may say that we just do not have enough faith or we have some big sin in our life or something we have done causes God to step away from us so we are not hearing His voice.

During the winter of the earth many events take place. Insects are destroyed; trees and flowers are renewed by increasing their root system and there is much needed rest for many animals. The earth is watered by the increased rain and melting snow. These are good things that happen even though, on the surface, it appears they are dead and nothing good is taking place.

Then it happens, days become warmer and warmer, flowers pop out of the ground, new growth is seen on the trees, birds appear back in the yard and the melodies of nature begin again. Spring is in the air. Once again birds build their nest, give birth to new babies, everything is a lush green again and soon the dead of winter is forgotten.

So it is in our spiritual life. We need periods of reflection. We need time for much needed rest. So why do we allow ourselves to get so depressed and down? We need to remember that God is there, even though we may not see Him. He is right there giving us time to reflect.

Psalms 77:1-15 says:

My voice rises to God, I will cry aloud;

My voice rises to God, and He will hear me.

In the day of my trouble I sought the Lord;

In the night my hand was stretched out without weariness;

My soul refused to be comforted.

When I remember God, then I am disturbed;

When I sigh, then my spirit grows faint.   Selah.

You have held my eyelids open;

I am so troubled that I cannot speak.

I have considered the days of old,

The years of long ago.

I will remember my song in the night; I will meditate with my heart,

And my spirit ponders:

Will the Lord reject forever?

And will He never be favorable again?

Has His lovingkindness ceased forever?

Has His promise come to an end forever?

Has God forgotten to be gracious?

Or has He in anger withdrawn His compassion?   *Selah.*

Then I said, "It is my grief,

That the right hand of the Most High has changed.

I shall remember the deeds of the Lord;

Surely I will remember Your wonders of old.

I will meditate on all Your work

And must muse on Your deeds.

Your way, O God, is holy;

What god is great like our God?

You are the God who works wonders;

You have made known Your strength among the peoples.

You have by Your power redeemed Your people,

The sons of Jacob and Joseph.   *Selah.*

We see here that David, finding himself in a time of winter, feeling like God could not be found, went back to the past and remembered all that God had done for him and His people.

Many times as we serve the Lord, we are growing and healthy, just like spring. We begin to produce fruit in our lives that bring glory to God. Then a time for winter comes and God begins to deal with us about certain things in our lives that are displeasing to Him. These are hard times. These are the times we sometimes get confused and wonder if we will ever get it right.

As we continue to pray and ask God to show us how to remove these things from our lives we slowly begin to change colors. We see desires for these "fleshly" things begin to decrease. Just as the sap goes down the trees and the leaves begin to fall, so these things begin to fall from our lives. As God continues the process of pruning in our life, these things are replaced by the fruit of the Spirit: love, joy, peace, patience, kindness, gentleness, goodness, faithfulness and self-control.

Suddenly the attitudes we once held are replaced by compassion for others. The desire to criticize others is replaced by the desire to pray for them and ask God to use us to touch their lives. The desire to argue and fight is replaced with the desire to be at peace with all men. The desire to go to certain places is changed to "where do you want me to go Lord?"

As these things begin to take root in our lives we begin to grow again and before you know it, spring is here and the process starts all over again.

As we experience times of "winter" in our lives we need to use it to spend time with the Lord. Ask Him to show us things in our life He is not pleased with. Ask Him to help us see our self the way He sees us and then ask Him to create in us a clean heart; on that is useful to Him and can produce the fruit that will last and bring Him Glory!

"Oh Lord, help us to recognize the seasons in our lives that You bring. Help us to be open to whatever it is You are trying to do and help us not allow Satan to rob us of the changes You want to make in us as we experience the seasons of our Christian walk. In Jesus Name, A-men."

"Weaker Vessel"
Put Down or Blessing?

I was leading a Precept Bible Study on Colossians and as we came to the end of Chapter 3 and into Chapter 4, we began talking about the scripture that instructs a wife to submit to her husband. As we were reviewing cross references to this scripture, we were taken to 1 Peter where he addresses the wife as the weaker vessel and this lead to some very interesting discussion. 1 Peter 3:7 says, *"Husbands, in the same way be considerate as you live with your wives, and treat them with respect as the weaker vessel and as heirs with you of the gracious gift of life, so that nothing will hinder your prayers."* (NASB)

In our class, we begin to talk about why Peter would call the wife the weaker vessel and some took offense to this thought. One statement was made that during this time women were thought to be inferior to men and were not really useful for anything except to bear children and work in the home.

As I began praying about this phrase "weaker vessel" several thoughts came to my mind and I began to do some investigating into the term and God began to show me some very interesting things.

This term weaker is the Greek word, 'Asthenes' which means more feeble, impotent, sick, without strength, weak. This word basically means without strength, powerless. In classic Greek it is never used with the meaning of moral weakness, but only in a physical sense, weak, powerless without ability.

As I pondered this for a moment, I began to think about where women and men came from and the makeup of their creation. As you recall, in Genesis 1:26 God said, **"Let us make man in Our own image, in Our likeness..."** (NASB) This statement alone makes both men and women are important in order to show the character of God. In Chapter 2 we are given specific details of this process. Verse 7 says, *"The Lord God formed man from the dust of the ground and breathed into his nostrils the breath of life and man became a living being."* (NASB)

Just think about it, a man was formed from the dust of the ground. The Hebrew word for dust here is 'Apar' and it means, dust, clods, plaster, and ashes. The dust of the ground along with gravity holds the world together. The dust is weak in and of itself, however when you add rock, clay and other materials you get a firm strong foundation on which to stand. We take the particles of dust, make bricks and use them to build buildings, etc. So no wonder man has strength, God created Him that way. However, man needs the Rock of Jesus in his life to really become what God wants him to be.

In Genesis 2:18, the Lord God said, *"It is not good for the man to be alone. I will make a helper suitable for him."* (NASB) God did not say, I will make him a slave in which to lord over or beat or take advantage of; but a helper, one who comes alongside the man to assist him. In Genesis 2:21-22 we find that God caused a deep sleep to fall on man and He took one of man's ribs and made the woman from the rib. How does the rib compare to the dust of the ground? The rib is a very slender, narrow piece of bone. Ribs are fragile. They are able to take minimal pressure however are very breakable when pressure is increased. The rib has an excellent purpose in that they protect the very vital parts of the body; the lungs and the heart. As we have already said the dust of the ground is strong, it is what we stand on so when you look at these two differences I would have to say that the rib is much weaker than the dust. Does this make the woman to be nothing? I dare say it does not.

When you look at the woman you see a unique creature created in God's image but different from the man. They are more tender, compassionate and emotional and need more attention. I believe this is the way God created them. Men are sterner, self-sufficient, goal oriented, and strong. He took the rib from the man's side, under his arm so he could protect the woman. Not from his head so she can lord over him or from his foot to be walked on but from his side to be comforted, nourished, cared for, protected and loved. Does this make women insignificant? Absolutely not! Remember the ribs, although fragile, play a major role in protecting the vital organs of the body. They are flexible in order to give way to minimal pressure. They are curved and not straight in order to wrap around the chest, however they are weak and can break under great pressure.

Women are the same way. They are created as the helper, not the leader. They are to nourish and care for the family; they are the ones who usually hold the family together. They are flexible in order to meet the demands of the home and this makes them a vital part of the family. They are weaker in some ways because they are easily swayed and easily deceived. Remember it was Eve that Satan went after in the garden and she was captivated by his persuasion and fell into his trap. She was then able to get her husband to also eat the forbidden fruit. Satan knew she could be tricked because that is the way she is created!

In 1 Corinthians 1:27 we are told, *"But God chose the foolish things to the world to shame the wise; God chose the weak things of the world to shame the strong."* (NASB) God chooses women, the weaker vessel to help accomplish His goals. Peter tells us in 1 Peter 3:1 that wives are to *"Be submissive to your own husbands so that even if any of them are disobedient to the word, they may be won without a word by the behavior of their wives as they observe your chaste and respectful behavior."* (NASB) He goes on to tell them to *"Let your beauty be from our inner self, the unfading beauty of a gentle and quite spirit, which is of great worth in God's sight"* (NASB). God never says He will use the man to change the woman but by the obedience of the woman He can change the man.